A collection of Tree Programming Interview Questions Solved in C++

Antonio Gulli

"Tree" is the fifth of a series of 25 Chapters devoted to algorithms, problem solving and C++ programming.

DEDICATION

To my wife Francesca

Love always finds a path between forgiveness and karma

ACKNOWLEDGMENTS

Table of Contents

1 Implementing preorder visit for a Binary Tree

Solution

A binary tree is a tree where every node has at most two children. The non-recursive pre-order visit can be implemented by using a stack. In a loop:

- First, the current node is visited.
- Then the left children are pushed until a leaf is reached
- Then if the stack is empty we leave the loop. Else the top of the stack is popped out and the visit continues towards the right children

Code

```cpp
template<typename tVal>
    struct binaryTree
    {
        tVal v__;
        struct binaryTree<tVal> * left;
        struct binaryTree<tVal> * right;

        binaryTree(tVal v) : v__(v),
            left(NULL), right(NULL) {}
    };

    template<typename tVal>
    void nonRecursivePreOrder(binaryTree<tVal> * root)
    {
        std::stack<binaryTree<tVal> *> s;

        while (true)
        {
            //left
            while (root)
            {
                std::cout << " v=" << root->v__;
                s.push(root);
                root = root->left;
            }
            if (s.empty())
                break;

            // this one
            root = s.top();
            s.pop();
```

```
        //right
        root = root->right;
    }
}
```

Complexity

Time complexity is $O(n)$ and space complexity is $O(n)$

2   Computing the diameter of a binary tree

Solution

The solution can be computed easily by recursion

Code

```
template<typename tVal>
    unsigned diameter(binaryTree<tVal> * root, unsigned & dim)
    {
        unsigned left, right;
        if (!root)
            return 0;

        left = diameter(root->left, dim);
        right = diameter(root->right, dim);
        if (left + right > dim)
            dim = left + right;
        return ((left > right) ? left : right) + 1;
    }
```

Complexity

Time complexity is $O(n)$ and space complexity is $O(n)$.

3   Implementing an inorder visit for a Binary Tree

Solution

A non-recursive in-order visit can be implemented by using a stack. In a loop:

- First, left children are pushed until a leaf is reached

- Then if the stack is empty, we leave the loop. Otherwise the top of the stack pops out and the current node is visited.
- Finally the visit continues towards the right children

Code

```cpp
template<typename tVal>
void nonRecursiveInOrder(binaryTree<tVal> * root)
{
    std::stack<binaryTree<tVal> *> s;

    while (true)
    {
        //left
        while (root)
        {
            s.push(root);
            root = root->left;
        }
        if (s.empty())
            break;

        // this one
        root = s.top();
        s.pop();

        std::cout << " v=" << root->v__;

        //right
        root = root->right;
    }
}
```

Complexity

Time complexity is $O(n)$ and space complexity is $O(n)$

4   Implementing a postorder visit for a Binary Tree

Solution

For post-ordering every single node is visited twice: the first time when moving towards the left children and then again, when moving towards the right children. For differentiating the two cases we can compare if the current element and the right child of the element at the top of the stack are the same.

Code

```cpp
template<typename tVal>
void nonRecursivePostOrder(binaryTree<tVal> * root)
{
    std::stack<binaryTree<tVal> *> s;

    while (true)
    {
        if (root)
        {
            s.push(root);
            root = root->left;
        }
        else {
            if (s.empty())
                break;
            else
                if (!s.top()->right)
                {
                    root = s.top();
                    s.pop();
                    std::cout << " v=" << root->v__;

                    if (root == s.top()->right)
                    {
                        std::cout << " v=" << s.top()->v__;
                        s.pop();
                    }
                }
            if (!s.empty())
                root = s.top()->right;
            else
                root = NULL;
        } // else
    } // while
}
```

Complexity

Time complexity is $O(n)$ and space complexity is $O(n)$

5   Implementing a level order visit for a Binary Tree

Solution

Level order visits can be implemented for all the nodes at one level before going to the next level. The idea is very simple.

In a loop:

- First, the root is visited
- Then while traversing nodes at level l all the nodes at level $l + 1$ are stored in a queue
- The loop is continued until all the levels are completed

Code

```cpp
template<typename tVal>
    void nonRecursiveLevelOrder(binaryTree<tVal> * root)
    {
        std::queue<binaryTree<tVal> *> q;
        binaryTree<tVal> * tmp;

        if (!root)
            return;

        q.push(root);
        while (!q.empty())
        {
            tmp = q.front();
            q.pop();
            std::cout << " v=" << tmp->v__;
            if (tmp->left)
                q.push(tmp->left);
            if (tmp->right)
                q.push(tmp->right);
        }
    }
```

Complexity

Time complexity is $O(n)$ and space complexity is $O(n)$.

6   Counting the number of leaves in a tree

Solution

A solution can be provided by modifying the level order visit where we increment a counter every time we reach a leaf node.

Code

```cpp
template<typename tVal>
    unsigned NumLeavesNonRecursiveLevelOrder(binaryTree<tVal> *
root)
    {
        std::queue<binaryTree<tVal> *> q;
        binaryTree<tVal> * tmp;

        unsigned count = 0;

        if (!root)
            return count;

        q.push(root);
        while (!q.empty())
        {
            tmp = q.front();
            q.pop();
            if (!tmp->left && !tmp->right)
            {
                count++; // another leaf
            }
            else
            {
                if (tmp->left)
                    q.push(tmp->left);
                if (tmp->right)
                    q.push(tmp->right);
            }
        }
        return count;
    }
```

Complexity

Time complexity is $O(n)$ and space complexity is $O(n)$.

7 Checking if two binary trees are structurally identical

Solution

A solution can be provided by recursion. We consider as base cases when both nodes are null, or if only one of them is null. Otherwise, the algorithm checks, if both nodes contain the same value and if both left children and right children are recursively structurally identical.

Code

```cpp
template<typename tVal>
    unsigned structIdentical(binaryTree<tVal> * r1,
binaryTree<tVal> * r2)
    {
        if (!r1 && !r2)
            return true;
        if (!r1 || !r2)
            return false;

        return (r1->v__ == r2->v__ &&
            structIdentical(r1->left, r2->left) &&
            structIdentical(r1->right, r2->right));

    }
```

Complexity

Time complexity is $O(n)$ and space complexity is $O(n)$.

8 Printing all the paths in a binary tree

Solution

A solution can be provided by recursion. The idea is to keep a vector v passing during recursion, while every node is pushed_back() to v. Every time we reach a leaf, the vector is printed.

Code

```cpp
template<typename tVal>
    void printAllPaths(binaryTree<tVal> * root,
        std::vector<tVal> path)
    {
        if (!root)
```

```
      return;
   path.push_back(root->v__);
   if (!root->left && !root->right)
   {
      std::vector<tVal>::iterator it = path.begin();
      for (; it != path.end(); it++)
         std::cout << " v=" << *it;
      std::cout << std::endl;
   }
   else
   {
      printAllPaths(root->left, path);
      printAllPaths(root->right, path);
   }
}
```

Complexity

Time complexity is $O(n)$ and space complexity is $O(n)$.

9   Verifying if a path sum is equal to an integer

Solution

The idea is to subtract the current value from the given sum, while visiting recursively the tree.

Code

```
template<typename tVal>
   bool hasSum(binaryTree<tVal> * root,
      int sum)
   {
      if (!root)
         return (sum == 0);
      else
      {
         int remainingSum = sum - root->v__;
         if ((root->left && root->right) ||
            (!root->left && !root->right))
            return (hasSum(root->left, remainingSum) ||
            hasSum(root->right, remainingSum));
         else
         if (root->left)
            return hasSum(root->left, remainingSum);
```

```
        else
            return hasSum(root->right, remainingSum);
    }
}
```

Complexity

Time complexity is $O(n)$ and space complexity is $O(n)$.

10 Find the maximum path sum between two leaves of a binary tree

Solution

The maximum path sum between two leaves can either touch the root of the three or can be located on subtree only of the tree. Hence we have the following cases of recursion:

- The base case is when the root is NULL and we return 0
- Then, we compute recursively the maximum path sum for left and right subtree respectively
- Then we compute the maximum for left subtree, for right subtree, and for the subtree rooted at the current node. If this maximum improves the total maximum observed so far, then the total maximum is updated
- Returning from recursion we compute the maximum between right and left subtrees and add the weight for the current node

Code

```
template<typename tVal>
    tVal max(tVal a, tVal b)
    {
        return (a >= b) ? a : b;
    }

    template<typename tVal>
    int maxPathSum(binaryTree<tVal> * root, tVal &res)
    {
        if (!root)
            return 0;

        int lLPSum = maxPathSum(root->left, res);
        int rLPSum = maxPathSum(root->right, res);
```

```
        int curr_sum = max((lLPSum + rLPSum + root->v__),
            max(lLPSum, rLPSum));
        if (res < curr_sum)
            res = curr_sum;
        return max(lLPSum, rLPSum) + root->v__;
    }
```

Complexity

The time complexity is $O(n)$ and space complexity is $O(n)$.

11   Reconstructing a tree given its pre-order and in-order traversals

Solution

In a preorder visit the root is always the leftmost element of each subtree. So we start to put the leftmost element of the preorder array of visit as the root of the whole tree. Now, if we search the that element in the inorder array we can immediately infer the all the elements that are before that value belong to the left subtree and all the elements after that value belong to the right subtree. The solution can therefore computed recursively.

Code

```
template<typename tVal>
unsigned search(std::vector<tVal> inorder,
    unsigned start, unsigned end, tVal v)
{
    for (unsigned i = start, i <= end; i__++)
        if (inorder[i] == v)
            return i;
}

template<typename tVal>
binaryTree<tVal> * buildBTfromInorderAndPreorder(
    const std::vector<tVal> & inOrder,
    const std::vector<tVal> & preOrder,
    unsigned & preIndex,
    unsigned inStart, unsigned inEnd)
{
    binaryTree<tVal> * n;
    n->v__ = preOrder[preIndex++];
```

```
    if (inStart == inEnd)
        return n;

    int inIndex =
        search(inOrder, inStart, inEnd, n->v__);
    n->left =
        buildBTfromInorderAndPreorder(inOrder, preOrder,
        inStart, inIndex - 1);
    n->right =
        buildBTfromInorderAndPreorder(inOrder, preOrder,
        inIndex+1, inEnd);
}
```

Complexity

The time complexity is $O(n^2)$. Question for the interested reader is whether or not this is the optimal complexity.

12 Printing a zig-zag traversal

Solution

Zig-Zag traversal is implemented by using two stacks which are swapped at every level. During the visit of *currentLevel* all the children are inserted in the *nextLevel* stack Also, a Boolean value is maintained for determining the direction of visit (either left to right, or right to left) and this direction in reversed at every cycle. Whe *currentLevel* stack is empty then it is swapped with *nextLevel*. By using two stacks zig-zag visit is a variant of level order visit.

Code

```
template<typename tVal>
void printZigZag(binaryTree<tVal> * root)
{
    binaryTree<tVal> * tmp;
    bool left2right = true;

    if (!root)
        return;

    std::stack<binaryTree<tVal> *> currLevel;
    std::stack<binaryTree<tVal> *> nextLevel;

    currLevel.push(root);
```

```
while (!currLevel.empty())
{
    tmp = currLevel.top();
    currLevel.pop();

    if (tmp)
    {
        std::cout << " v=" << tmp->v__;
        if (left2right)
        {
            nextLevel.push(tmp->left);
            nextLevel.push(tmp->right);
        }
        else
        {
            nextLevel.push(tmp->right);
            nextLevel.push(tmp->left);
        }
    }
    if (currLevel.empty())
    {
        left2right = !left2right;
        currLevel.swap(nextLevel);
    }
}
}
```

Complexity

The time complexity is $O(n)$ and space complexity is $O(n)$.

13 Printing the lowest common ancestor (LCA)

Solution

A solution can be computed recursively. The lowest common ancestor for two node $n1$ and $n2$ is $NULL$ if the root is $NULL$. Otherwise the LCA is $n1$ (respectively $n2$) if the root is $n1$ (respectively $n2$). Those are the base cases. Them recursively the solution is computed for left and for right subtree. After returning from recursion if both left and right are both available then the LCA is the current root, otherwise is left if this is available (respectively right, if this is available).

Code

```
template<typename tVal>
    binaryTree<tVal> * LCA(binaryTree<tVal> * root,
        binaryTree<tVal> * n1, binaryTree<tVal> * n2)
    {
        if (!root)
            return NULL;
        if (root == n1 || root == n2)
            return root;

        binaryTree<tVal> * left =
            LCA(root->left, n1, n2);

        binaryTree<tVal> * right =
            LCA(root->right, n1, n2);

        if (left && right)
            return root;
        else
            return (left ? left : right);
    }
```

Complexity

The time complexity is $O(n)$ and space complexity is $O(n)$.

14   Implementing find and insert in a Binary Search Tree

Solution

A Binary Search Tree (BST) is a tree where each node has no more than two children. The left subtree of a node contains only nodes with keys being strictly less than the node's key. The right subtree of a node contains only nodes with keys being greater than the node's key.

Find() begins by examining the *root node*. If the tree is null, the key does not exist in the tree. If the key equals the one of the root, *find()* returns the *root*. If the key is less than the one of the root, the left subtree is searched. If the key is greater than the one of the root, the right subtree is searched. This method is repeated recursively or iteratively. Here below we propose a recursive version and we leave to the interested reader the task of implementing an iterative version.

Insert() follows a similar approach. The candidate key for insertion is searched in the tree. If it is found, the process returns. Otherwise if the search reaches a null node, the key is inserted in that position. The process can be recursive or iterative.

Code

```
template<typename tVal>
    template<typename tVal>
struct binaryTree
{
    tVal v__;
    struct binaryTree<tVal> * left;
    struct binaryTree<tVal> * right;

    binaryTree(tVal v) : v__(v),
        left(NULL), right(NULL) {}
};

template<typename tVal>
binaryTree<tVal> * find(binaryTree<tVal> * const root,
    const tVal k)
{
    if (!root)
        return NULL;

    return ((root->v__ < k) ? find(root->right, k) :
        (root->v__ > k ? find(root->left, k) : root));
}

template<typename tVal>
void insert(binaryTree<tVal> * & root, const tVal k)
{
    if (!root)
    {
        root = new binaryTree<tVal>(k);
        return;
    }

    if (root->v__ < k)
        insert(root->right, k);
    else if (root->v__ > k)
        insert(root->left, k);
}
```

Complexity

Average time complexity of insert and find is $O(logn)$ where n expresses the number of nodes in the tree. However if the tree is not balanced, complexity is $O(n)$.

15   Print a BST in order

Solution

A BST is a binary tree, so the inorder visit starts with the left subtree , then by visiting the current node and finally the right subtree.

Code

```
template<typename tVal>
void printInorder(binaryTree<tVal> * const node)
{
    if (!node)
        return;

    printInorder(node->left);
    std::cout << " n=" << node->v__;
    printInorder(node->right);
}
```

Complexity

Time complexity is $O(n)$, where n is the number of nodes in the tree.

16   Implementing findMin and findMax in a BST

Solution

The minimum key is located in the leftmost children, while the maximum key is located in the rightmost children.

Code

```
template<typename tVal>
binaryTree<tVal> * findMin(binaryTree<tVal> * root)
{
    if (!root)
        return NULL;
```

```
    while (root->left) { root = root->left; }
    return root;
}

template<typename tVal>
binaryTree<tVal> * findMax(binaryTree<tVal> * root)
{
    if (!root)
        return NULL;
    while (root->right) { root = root->right; }
    return root;
}
```

Complexity

Average time complexity is $O(logn)$, where n is the number of nodes in the tree. However if the tree is not balanced, complexity is $O(n)$.

17   Implementing deleteNode in a BST

Solution

The code *deleteNode()* starts by finding the key to delete in the tree. If there is no key, the algorithm returns. Otherwise there are two different cases:

- If the node is internal, *deleteNode()* finds the maximum key in the left subtree rooted to the node, where the key has been found. This maximum key replaces the searched key, which is therefore removed. Then the maximum is deleted by the left subtree.

- If the node is external and there is on children (either on the left or on right side) then the child replaces the father In any case the external node is freed.

The following code implements the algorithm

Code

```
template<typename tVal>
   binaryTree<tVal> * deleteNode(binaryTree<tVal> * root,
      const tVal key)
   {
      binaryTree<tVal> * tmp;
      if (!root)
```

```
            return NULL;
      else if (key < root->v__)
          root->left = deleteNode(root->left, key);
      else if (key > root->v__)
          root->right = deleteNode(root->right, key);
      else {

          // internal node
          if (root->left && root->right)
          {
              tmp = findMax(root->left);
              root->v__ = tmp->v__;
              root->left = deleteNode(root->left, root->v__);
          }
          else
          {
              tmp = root;
              if (root->left == NULL)
                  root = root->right;
              if (root->right == NULL)
                  root = root->left;
              delete tmp;
          }
      }
      return root;
}
```

Complexity

Average time complexity is $O(\log n)$, where n is the number of nodes in the
tree. However if the tree is not balanced, complexity is $O(n)$.

18   Implementing the lowest common ancestor in a BST

Solution

The lowest common ancestor (LCA) of two nodes $n1$ (with key $k1$) and
$n2$ (with key $k2$) for a tree rooted at the *root* node is a node with key kn such
that either $k1 \leq kn \leq k2$ or $k1 \geq kn \geq k2$. If these conditions are not met,
LCA navigates the three by either moving left (if $k1 \leq kn$) or right, otherwise
until either the one of the conditions is met or an external node is reached.

Code

```
    template<typename tVal>
```

```
binaryTree<tVal> * lca(binaryTree<tVal> * const root,
    binaryTree<tVal> * const n1, binaryTree<tVal> * const n2)
{
    if (!root || !n1 || !n2)
        return;
    while (true)
    {
        if ((n1->v__ < root->v__) && (root->v__ < n2->v__ ) ||
            (n1->v__ > root->v__) && (root->v__ > n2->v__ ))
            return root;
        else if (n1->v__ < root->v__)
            root = root->left;
        else
            root = root->right;
    }
}
```

Complexity

The worst case time complexity is $O(n)$.

19 Check if a tree is a BST

Solution

A solution can be computed recursively by checking if the left subtree, the current node and the right subtree respect the BST ordering. It is therefore convenient to pass the previous analyzed key by reference and compare the current node with that key.

Code

```
template<typename tVal>
    bool isBST(binaryTree<tVal> *  const root,
        tVal & prev)
    {
        if (!root)
            return true;
        if (!isBST(root->left, prev))
            return false;
        if (root->v__ < prev)
            return false;
        prev = root->v__;
        return isBST(root->right, prev);
    }
```

Complexity

The worst case time complexity is $O(n)$.

20   Converting a Double linked list into a BST

Solution

Converting a double linked list into a BST can be easily achieved recursively. The forward pointer of the double linked list can be used as right child of a node and the backward pointer as left child. The algorithm starts by finding the element located in the middle position of the list (this is left as an exercise). This node is the root of the BST. Then the left side and the right side are computed recursively.

Code

```cpp
template<typename tVal>
struct dLL
{
    tVal v__;
    struct dLL<tVal> * prev;
    struct dLL<tVal> * next;

    dLL(tVal v) : v__(v),
        prev(NULL), next(NULL) {}
};


template <typename tVal>
dLL<tVal> * findMiddleNode(dLL<tVal> *head);

// left is prev
// right is next

template <typename tVal>
binaryTree<tVal> * doubleListToBST(dLL<tVal> * head)
{
    dLL<tVal> * tmp, * p, *q;

    // head and head->next exist
    if (!head || !head->next)
        return null;
```

```
    // find middle point
    tmp = findMiddleNode(head);

    // find the precedessor
    p = head;
    while (p->next != tmp)
        p = p->next;

    // break first half
    p->next = NULL;
    // start next half
    q = tmp->next;
    tmp->next = NULL;

    // recurisve
    tmp->prex = doubleListToBST(head);
    tmp->next = doubleListToBST(q);

    return tmp;
}
```

Complexity

Time complexity is $O(n)$, where n is the number of nodes in the list.

21   Converting a BST into a Double Linked List

Solution

Converting a BST into a double linked list can be easily achieved recursively. The right child of a node can be used as forward pointer of the double linked list and the left child as backward pointer. A special case happens at the beginning, when the *tail* pointer of the double linked list is not defined as detailed in the code.

Code

```
template <typename tVal>
void bstToDoubleList(binaryTree<tVal> *root,
    binaryTree<tVal> ** head, binaryTree<tVal> ** tail)
{
    if (!root)
        return;
```

```
    if (root->left)
        bstToDoubleList(root->left, head, tail);

    root->left = *tail;

    if (*tail)
        (*tail)->right = root;
    else
        *head = root;

    *tail = root;

    if (root->right)
        bstToDoubleList(root->right, head, tail);
};
```

Complexity

Time complexity is $O(n)$, where n is the number of nodes in the list.

22 Finding the k-th element in a BST

Solution

It is easy to solve the problem recursively by keeping a reference to a counter as explained in the code below.

Code

```
    template<typename tVal>
  binaryTree<tVal> * findkth(binaryTree<tVal> * const root,
      const tVal k, unsigned & count)
  {
      if (!root)
          return NULL;

      binaryTree<tVal> * left = findkth(root->left, k, count);
      if (left)
          return left;

      if (++count == k)
          return root;

      return findkth(root->right, k, count);
```

```
}
```

Complexity

Time complexity is $O(k)$, where k is the position of the key to be found.

23 Printing all the keys in a BST within a given interval

Solution

Given two keys k, h such that $k \leq h$, the BST tree is navigated so that if the current node has a key larger or equal than k, the navigation continues recursively with the left children. Then the range condition is checked and if it is met, the current node is printed. Finally the navigation continues recursively with the right children.

Code

```cpp
template<typename tVal>
binaryTree<tVal> * rangePrint(binaryTree<tVal> * const root,
    const tVal k, const tVal h)
{
    if (!root)
        return NULL;

    if (root->v__ >= k)
        rangePrint(root->left, k, h);

    if (root->v__ >= k && root->v__ <= h)
        std::cout << " v=" << root->v__;

    if (root->v__ <= h)
        rangePrint(root->right, k, h);
}
```

Complexity

The worst time complexity is $O(n)$, where n is the number of nodes in the tree.

24 Merge Two Balanced Binary Search Trees

Solution

The most efficient method for merging two BST is to store each of them in an array. Then the two sorted arrays are merged and the resulting array is converted back to a new BST.

Code

```cpp
template<typename tVal>
void storeInorder(binaryTree<tVal> * const root,
    std::vector<tVal> & inorder)
{
    if (!root)
        return;

    storeInorder(root->left, inorder);
    inorder.push_back(root->v__);
    storeInorder(root->right, inorder);
}

template<typename tVal>
void dumpVector(const std::vector<tVal> &v1)
{
    std::cout << std::endl;

    std::vector<tVal>::const_iterator it = v1.begin();
    for (; it != v1.end(); it++)
        std::cout << *it << " ";

    std::cout << std::endl;
}

template<typename tVal>
void merge(const std::vector<tVal> & v1,
    const std::vector<tVal> & v2,
    std::vector<tVal> & merged)
{
    unsigned m = v1.size(), n = v2.size();
    if (merged.size() != n + m)
        return;

    unsigned i = 0, j = 0, k = 0;

    while (i < m && j < n)
    {
```

```cpp
        if (v1[i] < v2[j])
            merged[k] = v1[i++];
        else
            merged[k] = v2[j++];
        k++;
    }

    while (i < m)
        merged[k++] = v1[i++];

    while (j < n)
        merged[k++] = v2[j++];
}

template<typename tVal>
binaryTree<tVal> * sortedArrayToBST(const std::vector<tVal>
&v,
    int start, int end)
{
    if (start > end)
        return NULL;

    int mid = (start + end) / 2;
    binaryTree<tVal> *root =
        new binaryTree<tVal>(v[mid]);

    root->left = sortedArrayToBST(v, start, mid - 1);
    root->right = sortedArrayToBST(v, mid + 1, end);

    return root;
}


template<typename tVal>
binaryTree<tVal> * mergeTrees(binaryTree<tVal> * const
root1,
    binaryTree<tVal>  * const root2)
{
    std::vector<int> v1;
    storeInorder(root1, v1);

    std::vector<int> v2;
    storeInorder(root2, v2);

    std::vector<int> merged(v1.size() + v2.size());
    merge(v1, v2, merged);
```

```
        dumpVector(merged);

        return sortedArrayToBST(merged, 0, merged.size() - 1);
    }

    template<typename tVal>
    void dump(binaryTree<tVal> * const root)
    {
        if (!root)
            return;
        else
            std::cerr << " v==" << root->v__ << " ";

        if (root->left)
        {
            std::cerr << " ->left ";
            dump(root->left);
        }

        if (root->right)
        {
            std::cerr << " ->right ";
            dump(root->right);
        }
    }
}
```

Complexity

This method has complexity $(n + m)$, where n and m are the numbers of nodes in the two BSTs.

25   Find if there is a triplet in a Balanced BST that adds to zero

Solution

The optimal solution is to convert the BST into a double linked list. Then it is possible to iterate through the list and for each negative element we try to find a pair in the list with sum equal to the key of the current node multiplied by -1.

Code

```
    template <typename tVal>
    void bstToDoubleList(binaryTree<tVal> *root,
        binaryTree<tVal> ** head, binaryTree<tVal> ** tail)
```

```cpp
{
    if (!root)
        return;

    if (root->left)
        bstToDoubleList(root->left, head, tail);

    root->left = *tail;

    if (*tail)
        (*tail)->right = root;
    else
        *head = root;

    *tail = root;

    if (root->right)
        bstToDoubleList(root->right, head, tail);
};

template <typename tVal>
bool isPresentInDLL(binaryTree<tVal> * head,
    binaryTree<tVal> * tail, int sum)
{
    while (head != tail)
    {
        int curr = head->v__ + tail->v__;
        if (curr == sum)
            return true;
        else if (curr > sum)
            tail = tail->left;
        else
            head = head->right;
    }
    return false;
}

template <typename tVal>
bool isTripletPresent(binaryTree<tVal> *root)
{
    if (!root)
        return false;

    binaryTree<tVal>* head = NULL;
    binaryTree<tVal>* tail = NULL;
    bstToDoubleList(root, &head, &tail);
```

```
    while ((head->right != tail) && (head->v__ < 0))
    {
        if (isPresentInDLL(head->right, tail, -1 * head->v__))
            return true;
        else
            head = head->right;
    }
    return false;
}
```

Complexity

This part is left to the reader as an exercise

26   Implementing a B-Tree

Solution

A b-tree allows insertion and deletion in logarithmic time and it is typically used for systems that write and read large blocks of data such as databases or file systems.

In B-trees internal nodes have a variable number of children nodes within a predefined range $(t, 2t]$. When data is inserted or removed from a node, its number of children nodes changes and therefore internal nodes may be joined or split for guaranteeing that they don't exceed the range. Each internal node of a B-tree will contain a number of sorted keys. The keys act as separation values which divide its subtree as explained in the figure. Therefore $t + 1$ is the minimum branching factor for the tree.

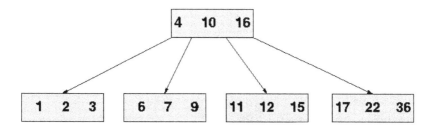

The factor of 2 will guarantee that nodes can be split or combined. If an internal node has $2d$ keys, then adding a key to that node can be accomplished by splitting the $2d$ key node into two d key nodes and by adding the key to the parent. Each split node maintains the required minimum number of keys. Likewise if an internal node and its neighbor each have d keys, then a key can be deleted from the internal node by joining with its neighbor. Deleting the key would leave $d-1$ keys to the internal node but joining the neighbor would add d keys plus one more key coming from the neighbor's parent. The total is still $2d$ keys. The number of branches from a node is one more than the number of keys stored in that node. A B-tree is kept balanced by requiring that all leaf-nodes are at the same depth.

More formally a B-tree of order $2t$ is defined as a tree which satisfies the following properties:
1. Every node has at most $2t$ children.
2. Every non-leaf node (except root) has at least t children.
3. The root has at least two children if it is not a leaf node.
4. A non-leaf node with k children contains $k-1$ keys.
5. All leaves appear in the same level
6. Each internal node's keys act as a separation value which divides its subtrees.

It can be shown that a b-tree of height h with all its nodes completely filled has $n = m^h - 1$ keys. The height of the B-tree is therefore $log_m(n+1)$ and this value makes the insert, logarithmically finds and deletes operations in the worst case

Search

This operation is similar to the one of searching a binary search tree. Starting at the root, the tree is recursively traversed from top to bottom and at each level the search chooses the subtree whose separation keys are on both sides of the search value. The search within a node can be linear or binary.

Insertion

To insert a new key, search the tree to find the leaf node, where the new key should be added:
- If the node contains fewer than t, then there is room for the new element, which can be inserted by respecting the order.
- Otherwise if the node is full and it must be split it into two nodes:
  - The median element is selected among the leaf's elements and the new element.

- Values less than the median one are put in the new left node and values greater than the median one are put in the new right node
- The median acts as a separation value.

The separation key is inserted in the node's parent, which should be split, if full. If the node is the root, we need to create a new root above the old one.

If the splitting goes all the way up to the root, it creates a new root with a single separator key and two children. When a node is split, one key goes to the parent, but one additional key is added.

Deletion

The idea is to find and delete the item, then restructure the tree to regain its invariants. This operation is left as an exercise.

Code

```cpp
#ifndef BTREE_HEAD_
#define BTREE_HEAD_ 1
#include <iostream>

namespace Tree{

    typedef int tKey;

    class BtreeNode;
    typedef BtreeNode * BtreeLink;

    class BtreeNode
    {
    private:
        unsigned t__; // 2t-1 keys, 2t children
        bool leaf__;  // is a leaf
        unsigned n__; // current number
        tKey * keys__;     // array of key
        BtreeLink * children__; // ptr to array of children

    public:

        // constructor
        BtreeNode(unsigned t, bool leaf) :
            t__(t), leaf__(leaf), n__(0),
            keys__(new tKey[2 * t__ - 1]),
            children__(new BtreeLink[2 * t__])
        {};
```

```cpp
// traverse
void traverse(unsigned lev=0)
{
    std::cout << "lev=" << lev << " ";

    // n keys, n+1 childrens
    unsigned i = 0;
    for (; i < n__; i++)
    {
        std::cout << " " << keys__[i];

        if (!leaf__)
            children__[i]->traverse(lev+1);
    }
    // last children
    if (!leaf__)
        children__[i]->traverse(lev + 1);
};

// delete all
void deleteAll()
{
    //n+1 children
    for (unsigned i = 0; i <= n__; i++)
    {
        if (!leaf__)
            children__[i]->deleteAll();
    }
    delete[] children__;
    delete[] keys__;
};

// dstrc
~BtreeNode()
{
    deleteAll();
}

// search in btree
//
BtreeLink search(tKey k)
{
    unsigned i = 0;
    // search right location
    for (; i < n__ && k > keys__[i]; i++);
```

```cpp
        // found the key
        if (keys__[i] == k)
            return this;

        // not found
        if (leaf__)
            return NULL;

        // recursively
        return children__[i]->search(k);
}

// insert in a node that is not full

void insertNonFull(tKey k)
{
    // rightmost key
    int i = n__ - 1;

    if (leaf__)
    {
        // one position is available
        // so copy the keys and
        // find the right spot
        while (i >= 0 && keys__[i] > k)
        {
            keys__[i + 1] = keys__[i];
            i--;
        }
        // found the right position
        keys__[i + 1] = k;
        n__++;
    }
    else // non leaf
    {
        // find the right spot
        while (i >= 0 && keys__[i] > k)
            i--;

        // full
        // split and recursively insert
        if (children__[i + 1]->n__ == 2 * t__ - 1)
        {
            splitChild(i + 1, children__[i + 1]);

            if (keys__[i + 1] < k)
                i++; // next children
        }
```

```cpp
            children__[i + 1]->insertNonFull(k);
        }

        std::cout << "traversing n==" << n__;
        traverse();
        std::cout << std::endl;
    }

    void splitChild(int i, BtreeLink l)
    {
        BtreeLink m = new BtreeNode(l->t__, l->leaf__);
        m->n__ = t__ - 1;

        // copy the right keys from t to 2t-1
        for (unsigned j = 0; j < t__ - 1; j++)
            m->keys__[j] = l->keys__[j + t__];

        // copy the children from t to 2t
        if (!l->leaf__)
        {
            for (unsigned j = 0; j < t__ ; j++)
                m->children__[j] = l->children__[j + t__];
        }
        // one key less
        l->n__ = t__ - 1;

        // make room
        for (int j = n__ ; j >= i+1; j--)
            children__[j + 1] = children__[j];

        // connect the new node
        children__[i + 1] = m;

        // make room
        for (int j = n__ - 1; j >= i; j--)
            keys__[j + 1] = keys__[j];

        //copy the middle key
        keys__[i] = l->keys__[t__ - 1];

        n__++;
    }

    friend class Btree;
};
```

```cpp
class Btree
{
   BtreeNode * root;
   unsigned t__;

public:

   Btree(unsigned t) :
      root(NULL), t__(t) {};

   void traverse()
   {
      if(root) root->traverse();
   }

   BtreeLink search(tKey k)
   {
      return(root ? root->search(k) : NULL);
   }

   void insert(tKey k)
   {
      if (!root)
      {
         root = new BtreeNode(t__, true);
         root->keys__[0] = k;
         root->n__ = 1;
      }
      else
      {
         // full root
         if (root->n__ == 2 * t__ - 1)
         {
            BtreeLink btn = new BtreeNode(t__, false);
            btn->children__[0] = root;

            // split the root
            // move 1 key to one children
            btn->splitChild(0, root);

            if (btn->keys__[0] < k)
               btn->children__[1]->insertNonFull(k);
            else
               btn->children__[0]->insertNonFull(k);

            // change root
            root = btn;
         }
```

```
        else
            root->insertNonFull(k);
    }

    }
    };
};
#endif
```

Complexity

The table here below provides space complexity for the average and the worst case. In addition space and time complexity for search, insert and delete are also reported.

	Average case	Worst case
Space	$O(n)$	$O(n)$
Search	$O(logn)$	$O(logn)$
Insert	$O(logn)$	$O(logn)$
Delete	$O(logn)$	$O(logn)$

27   Implementing a Skiplist

Solution

Skiplists allow to find elements in a list with an average logarithmic time. The idea is to maintain additional pointers which allow to skip elements as in the image.

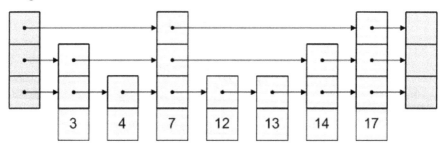

A skip list has many layers. The bottom layer is an ordinary ordered list. Each higher layer acts as "fast lane" for the lists below. In particular: an element in the i layer appears in the $i + 1$ layer with some probability p (typically p=0.5). On average each element appears in $1/(1 - p)$ lists, and the more frequent element in $log_{1/p} n$ lists.

Code

```
#ifndef SKIP_HEAD_
#define SKIP_HEAD_
#include <iostream>
#define DEBUG2 1

namespace Tree{

    typedef int num;

    template <typename Tkey, typename Tval>
    class Skiplist{

    private:

        struct node
        {
            Tkey key_;              // the key
            Tval val_;              // the val
            num size_;              // size of array
            node **next_;           // array of pointers

            node(const Tkey key, const Tval val, num size) :
                key_(key), val_(val), size_(size), next_(new
node*[size_])
            {
                for (num i = 0; i < size_; ++i) next_[i] = 0;
            }

        };

        typedef node* const link;

        Tkey default_key_;          // default item in skiplist
        Tval default_val_;          // default val in skiplist
        link head_;                 // head of skiplist

        num lgN_;                   // current number of link in
skiplist
```

```
      num lgNmax_;                    // max number of link in skiplist

      // random skiplist expansion
      num rand_sl_gen__()
      {
         num i, j, t = rand();   // t is in [0, RAND_MAX]

         // generate j=2, 4, ... i < lgNmax_
         // t > RAND_MAX / 2^i
         for (i = 1, j = 2; i < lgNmax_; i++, j += j)
            if (t > RAND_MAX / j) break;
         // t is a number < 1/2^i
         if (i > lgN_) // expand current level
            lgN_ = i; // this grows logaritimcally

         return i;
      }

      // remove a key and a val
      void remove__(link t, Tkey key, num k)
      {
#ifdef DEBUG2
         std::cerr << "remove__ " << t << " key="
            << key << " level=" << k << std::endl;
#endif
         if (t == 0) return;  // null?
         link x = t->next_[k];// next cell

         if ((x != 0) &&     // not null
            (x->key_ >= key))  // >=
         {
            if (key == x->key_){  // found it
               t->next_[k] = x->next_[k]; //    remove
#ifdef DEBUG2
               std::cerr << " done" << std::endl;
#endif
            }
            if (k == 0)  // can delete
            {               //   no more links in level
               delete x;
               return;
            }
            // try to remove one level below
            remove__(t, key, k - 1);
            return;
         }
```

```cpp
            // x->key_ < key
            // try to remove in the same level
            remove__(t->next_[k], key, k);
        }

        // remove all keys
        void remove_all__(link t, num k)
        {
#ifdef DEBUG
            std::cerr << "remove__ " << t << " level="
                << k << std::endl;
#endif
            if (t == 0) return;
            link x = t->next_[k];

            if (x != 0)
            {
                t->next_[k] = x->next_[k];    //    remove

                // can delete
                if (k == 0)
                {    //    no more links in level
                    delete x;
                    return;
                }
                // try to remove one level below
                remove_all__(t, k - 1);
            }
            // x->key_ >= key
            // try to remove in the same level
            remove_all__(t->next_[k], k);
        }

        // search a key, given a link and the current level
        Tval search__(link t, const Tkey key, num k) const
        {
#ifdef DEBUG
            std::cerr << "search__ " << t << " key="
                << key << " level=" << k << std::endl;
#endif
            if (t == 0)   // search failed
                return default_val_;
#ifdef DEBUG
            std::cerr << "key =" << key << " val = "
                << t->val_ << std::endl;
#endif
            if (key == t->key_) // search success
                return t->val_;
```

```cpp
        link x = t->next_[k]; // link to the next level
        if ((x == 0) ||        //   null?
            (key < x->key_))  //   search key < next level
link's key
        {
            if (k == 0) // no more levels available
                return default_val_;

            // try previous level
            return search__(t, key, k - 1);
        }
        // key > x->key_
        //   keep searching on the same level
        return search__(x, key, k);
    }

    // insert the new node pointed by link x with level k
    void insert__(link t, link x, num k)
    {
#ifdef DEBUG
        std::cerr << "insert__ " << t << " " << x << " level="
<< k
            << " key=" << x->key_ << " value=" << x->val_ <<
std::endl;
#endif

        Tkey key = x->key_;      // current key
        link tk = t->next_[k];   // link to next level current
link

        if ((tk == 0) ||         //   null?
            (key < tk->key_))   //   search key < next level
link's key
        {
            if (k < x->size_)  // is curr lev allowed for this
node?
            {                     //   insert:
                x->next_[k] = tk;// new node's successor is tk
                t->next_[k] = x; // t'successor is x
#ifdef DEBUG
                std::cerr << "\tdone inserted key=" << key
                    << " value=" << x->val_ << std::endl;
#endif
            }
            if (k == 0)              // level 0
```

```cpp
                return;                  //    return

                // k >= x->size__
                //   insert down a level
                insert__(t, x, k - 1);
                return;
            }
            // k > tk->key_
            insert__(tk, x, k);          //    stay in the same level
        }

    public:

        Skiplist(num lgNmax = 5) :
            head_(new node(default_key_, default_val_, lgNmax +
1)),
            lgN_(0), lgNmax_(lgNmax) {};

        ~Skiplist(){ remove_all__(head_, lgN_); };

        // search a key and get a val
        //    start from head_ and current level reached lgN_
        inline Tval search(const Tkey key) const
        {
            return search__(head_, key, lgN_);
        };

        // insert a key and a val
        // start from head_ and
        // the new randomized node with
        //    j=rand_sl_gen() links built with
        //    probability 1/t^j current level is lgN_
        //
        inline void insert(const Tkey key, const Tval val)
        {
            insert__(head_, new node(key, val, rand_sl_gen__()),
lgN_);
        };

        inline void remove(Tkey key)
        {
            remove__(head_, key, lgN_ -1);
        }
    }; // end class Skiplist

}; // end namespace Tree
```

```
#endif
```

Complexity

The table here below provides space complexity for the average and the worst cases. In addition space and time complexity for search, insert and delete is also reported.

	Average case	Worst case
Space	$O(n)$	$O(nlogn)$
Search	$O(logn)$	$O(n)$
Insert	$O(logn)$	$O(n)$
Delete	$O(logn)$	$O(n)$

28   Implementing Tries

Solution

A trie is an ordered tree data structure used to store dynamic set or associative array, where the keys are usually strings. Typically the strings are not explicitly memorized, instead each key has a position in the tree, which defines the key with which the position is associated. All the descendants of a node have a common prefix of the string associated with that node, and the root is associated with the empty string. In the example below the trie works for an alphabet of 26 different symbols and the position of each child identifies the current symbol for the inserted string. An example is provided in the image.

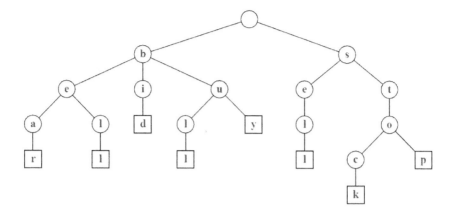

Code

```
ifndef TRIE_HEAD_
#define TRIE_HEAD_ 1
#include <iostream>
// suppose the trie is for 26 chars only
#define BRANCHLEVEL 26

namespace Tree{

    // this trie is used to memorize keys implicitely

    template <typename Tkey>
    class Trie{

    private:

        // a node contains a ptr to array of nodes
        struct node
        {
            // branch for this node
            node **next;
            node() : next(new node*[BRANCHLEVEL])
            {
                for (unsigned int i = 0; i < BRANCHLEVEL; i++)
                    next[i] = NULL;
            }
        };
        typedef node *link;
        link head;      // the head

        //recursive deletion of nodes
        //
```

```
void deleteTrie__(link l)
{
    if (!l)
        return;
    else
    {
        for (unsigned int i = 0; i < BRANCHLEVEL; i++)
            deleteTrie__(l->next[i]);
        delete[] l;
    }
}

// specialized version for Tkey == std::string
// this is equivalent to hash each letter
//
unsigned digit(std::string & k, unsigned d)
{
    if (d < k.length())
        return k[d] % BRANCHLEVEL;
    else
        return BRANCHLEVEL;
}

// search the key k from link l ed digit d
bool search__(link l, Tkey k, unsigned d)
{
    // get the d-th branch value from k
    unsigned int i = digit(k, d);
    if (i == BRANCHLEVEL) // found
        return true;
    if (!l)
        return false;

    // i-th branch in the tree
    return search__(l->next[i], k, d + 1);
}

// recursively insert considering the key
void insert__(link& l, Tkey k, unsigned d)
{
    // get the d-th branch value from k
    unsigned int i = digit(k, d);

    if (i == BRANCHLEVEL)
        return;
    if (!l)
```

```
            l = new node();
        insert__(l->next[i], k, d + 1);
    }

public:

    Trie() : head(NULL) {};
    ~Trie()
    {
        deleteTrie__(head);
    }

    bool search(Tkey k)
    {
        return search__(head, k, 0);
    }

    void insert(Tkey k)
    {
        insert__(head, k, 0);
    }

}; // end class Trie
}; // end namespace Tree

#endif
```

29   Implementing a segment tree

Solution

Given an $array[0, n-1]$, a segment tree allows:

a) to find the sum of elements in the range $[l, r]$ where $0 \le l \le r \le n - 1$ in time $O(logn)$

b) To update a specific element $array[i]$ such that $0 \le i \le n - 1$

Segment trees have the following properties

- Leaf nodes are the elements of $array$
- Each internal node represents a merge operation of the leaf nodes. Different types of problems have different representations of merge operations. In the code below we simply use a merge operation which sum all the leaves under the node

Frequently segment trees are represented in an array where for each node i the left child is in position $2i + 1$ and right child is in position $2 * i + 2$

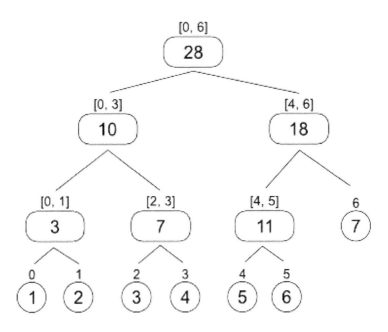

Code

```
inline int getMid(int s, int e)
{ return s + (e - s) / 2; }

    int getSumUtil(const int segmentTree[], int segmentStart,
int segmentEnd,
        int queryStart, int queryEnd, int index)
    {
        // contained in the interval
        if (queryStart <= segmentStart && segmentEnd <= queryEnd)
            return segmentTree[index];

        // If outside interval
        if (segmentEnd < queryStart || segmentStart > queryEnd)
            return 0;

        // If a part of this segment overlaps with the given
range
```

```
        unsigned mid = getMid(segmentStart, segmentEnd);

        // get the mid point and go left and right in the
segmentTree
        return getSumUtil(segmentTree, segmentStart, mid,
            queryStart, queryEnd, 2 * index + 1) +
          getSumUtil(segmentTree, mid + 1, segmentEnd,
            queryStart, queryEnd, 2 * index + 2);
    }

    void updateValueUtil(int segmentTree[], int segmentStart,
int segmentEnd,
        int whereToUpdate, int valueToAdd, int index)
    {
        // not the right interval
        if (whereToUpdate < segmentStart ||
           whereToUpdate > segmentEnd)
            return;

        // update
        segmentTree[index] += valueToAdd;
        if (segmentEnd != segmentStart)
        {
            // recursively get mid point and go left or right
            int mid = getMid(segmentStart, segmentEnd);
            updateValueUtil(segmentTree, segmentStart, mid,
                whereToUpdate, valueToAdd, 2 * index + 1);
            updateValueUtil(segmentTree, mid + 1, segmentEnd,
                whereToUpdate, valueToAdd, 2 * index + 2);
        }
    }

    void updateValue(int array[], int segmentTree[], int n,
        int whereToAdd, int newValue)
    {
        if (whereToAdd < 0 || whereToAdd > n - 1)
            return;

        int diff = newValue - array[whereToAdd];

        array[whereToAdd] = newValue;

        updateValueUtil(segmentTree, 0, n - 1,
            whereToAdd, diff, 0);
    }

    int getSum(int segmentTree[], int n,
        int queryStart, int queryEnd)
```

```cpp
{
    // Check for erroneous input values
    if (queryStart < 0 || queryEnd > n - 1 ||
        queryStart > queryEnd)
        return -1;

    return getSumUtil(segmentTree, 0, n - 1,
        queryStart, queryEnd, 0);
}

int constructSTUtil(const int array[], int segmentTree[],
    int segmentStart, int segmentEnd, int segmentIndex)
{
    if (segmentStart == segmentEnd)
    {
        segmentTree[segmentIndex] = array[segmentStart];
        return array[segmentStart];
    }

    int mid = getMid(segmentStart, segmentEnd);
    segmentTree[segmentIndex] =
        constructSTUtil(array, segmentTree,
            segmentStart, mid, segmentIndex * 2 + 1) +
        constructSTUtil(array, segmentTree,
            mid + 1, segmentEnd, segmentIndex * 2 + 2);
    return segmentTree[segmentIndex];
}

int *constructSegmentTree(int array[], int n)
{
    int x = (int)(ceil(log2(n))); //Height of segment tree
    int max_size = 2 * (int)pow(2, x) - 1; //Maximum size of
segment tree
    int *segmentTree = new int[max_size];

    constructSTUtil(array, segmentTree, 0, n - 1, 0);

    return segmentTree;
}
```

Complexity

Time complexity is $O(logn)$ for both update and range sum operations.

30   Implementing Range minimum queries

Solution

Given an $array[0, n-1]$, a segment tree allows to find the minimum in the range $[l, r]$ where $0 \le l \le r \le n - 1$ in time $O(logn)$. In this case the segment tree has the following properties

- Leaf nodes are the elements of $array$
- Each internal node represents the minimum all the leaves under the node

Frequently segment trees are represented in an array where for each node i the left child is in position $2i + 1$ and right child is in position $2 * i + 2$

Code

Left as an exercise

Complexity

Minimum is computed with $O(logn)$ time complexity. However, there is an $O(n)$ preprocessing time and $O(n)$ extra space required.

31   Implementing suffix tree

Solution

Suffix Tree (also known as Pat Tree) is a tree containing all the suffixes of a given string S. The construction of a suffix tree takes linear time and also linear space (although with very large constants). Once the suffix three is built it is possible to solve a myriad of problems on textual strings[1] such as:

- Check if a string P if length m is a substring of S in $O(m)$ time
- Find the longest common substrings of strings Si and Sj in $O(ni + nj)$ time

The list is very long and cannot be reported here. The interested reader can find these articles relevant

- http://www.di.unipi.it/~grossi/IND/survey.pdf

---

[1] http://en.wikipedia.org/wiki/Suffix_tree

- http://www.inf.fu-
  berlin.de/lehre/WS02/ALP3/material/sufficTree.pdf

The suffix tree for the string S of length n is defined as a tree such that:
- The tree has exactly n leaves
- Every internal node has at least two children, with the only exception of the root
- Each edge is labeled with a non-empty substring of S
- It is not allowed to have two edges starting out of a node with labels beginning with the same character
- The string obtained by concatenating all the labels on the path from the root to leaf i represents the suffix $S[i..n]$, $1 \leq i \leq n$

S is padded with a terminal symbol not seen in the string (usually denoted $\$$). This ensures that no suffix is a prefix of another.

string S = | m | i | s | s | i | s | s | i | p | p | i |
            1 2 3 4 5 6 7 8 9 10 11

(a) Suffix Trie

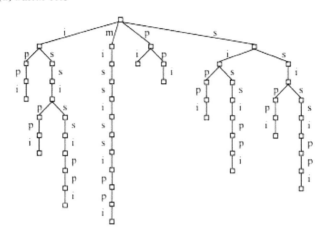

(b) Suffix Tree

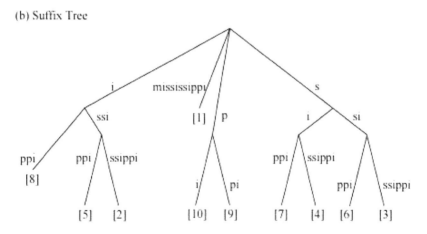

Code

The interested reader can access these libraries:

- http://codingplayground.blogspot.de/2010/05/suffix-tree-with-unicode-support.html
- https://code.google.com/p/patl/

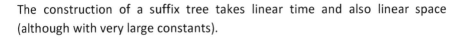

Complexity

The construction of a suffix tree takes linear time and also linear space (although with very large constants).

ABOUT THE AUTHOR

An experienced data mining engineer, passionate about technology and innovation in consumers' space. Interested in search and machine learning on massive dataset with a particular focus on query analysis, suggestions, entities, personalization, freshness and universal ranking. Antonio Gullì has worked in small startups, medium (Ask.com, Tiscali) and large corporations (Microsoft, RELX). His carrier path is about mixing industry with academic experience.

Antonio holds a Master Degree in Computer Science and a Master Degree in Engineering, and a Ph.D. in Computer Science. He founded two startups, one of them was one of the earliest search engine in Europe back in 1998. He filed more than 20 patents in search, machine learning and distributed system. Antonio wrote several books on algorithms and currently he serves as (Senior) Program Committee member in many international conferences. Antonio teaches also computer science and video game programming to hundreds of youngsters on a voluntary basis.

"Nowadays, you must have a great combination of research skills and a just-get-it-done attitude."